"If you believe in yourself and have the courage, the determination, the dedication, the competitive drive, and if you are willing to sacrifice the little things in life and pay the price for the things that are worthwhile, it can be done."

"Mental toughness is many things and rather difficult to explain. Its qualities are sacrifice and self-denial. Also, most importantly, it is combined with a perfectly disciplined will that refuses to give in. It's a state of mind—you could call it character in action."

The Lombardi Rules

26 Lessons from Vince Lombardi—the World's Greatest Coach

VINCE LOMBARDI, JR.

MCGRAW-HILL

New York   Chicago   San Francisco   Lisbon
London   Madrid   Mexico City   Milan   New Delhi
San Juan   Seoul   Singapore   Sydney   Toronto

4 5 6 7 8 9 0 DOC/DOC 0 1 9 8 7 6 5

ISBN 0-07-144489-0

Printed and bound by RR Donnelley.

McGraw-Hill books are available at special quantity discounts to use as premiums and sales promotions, or for use in corporate training programs. For more information, please write to the Director of Special Sales, McGraw-Hill Professional, Two Penn Plaza, New York, NY 10121-2298. Or contact your local bookstore.

Contents

☑ The Lombardi Rules

A leadership book from a football coach?

My father, Vince Lombardi, was not a captain of industry. He didn't run a multi-billion dollar organization, and he never wrote books on business strategy. He was, simply, a very successful football coach. He tried to be other things—he began his career teaching high school physics, chemistry, and Latin, in addition to coaching football and basketball—but soon found his true calling lay in exhorting others to greatness on the football field.

As coach of the Green Bay Packers from 1959 to 1967, Lombardi took a ragtag group of players that had floundered at the bottom of the National Football League for years, and—in only two seasons—molded them into a championship team. The Packers won NFL championships in 1961, 1962, and 1965, as well as the first two Super Bowls in 1966 and 1967. His brilliance as a coach became legendary, and his fame quickly spread from Green Bay, Wisconsin, to the rest of the country.

But how does this relate to business? How do Vince Lombardi's winning ways on the football field apply to the corporate boardroom and the shopfloor to leaders who strive to make their organizations excellent? What does winning a football game have to do with closing a deal?

The answer lies less in *what* Lombardi achieved, and more in *how* he achieved it. My father was not only a great football coach; he was also a great *leader*.

It was his leadership—his ability to motivate his players, to inspire them to surpass their own perceived physical and mental capability, and his incredible will to win—that brought the nickname "Titletown, USA" to a small industrial city in Wisconsin, and brought national renown to the man, his methods, and his players.

Lombardi had definite ideas about the qualities and tactics required for effective leadership. In the Lombardi model, leadership starts with a simple premise: *Only by knowing yourself can you become an effective leader*. Once you understand yourself, you can start to grow and write your character, building the crucial attributes of a leader, such as character and integrity. Once these are developed, the building blocks are in place for you to become a successful leader.

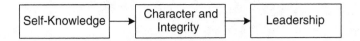

Self-Knowledge → Character and Integrity → Leadership

This philosophy is presented in this book through 26 lessons in leadership, following the model laid out above. These techniques helped my father and the Packers be number 1 on the football field, and I believe that they can help you and your organization be number 1 in *your* field.

And they can do more. Lombardi's leadership model is about finishing first, but it's also about being a person of character, finishing what you start, never compromising your goals, and giving everything you've got to achieve your goals.

"Leadership rests not only on outstanding ability but on commitment, loyalty, pride, and followers ready to accept guidance."

☐ Ask Others Tough
~~Questions~~

☑ Ask Yourself Tough Questions

The Lombardi code is founded on the belief that you can only become a leader after developing your character—that is, after building integrity, honesty, and commitment. The way to develop these attributes is through self-knowledge. You can't improve what you don't understand.

The first steps on the road to self-knowledge involve asking ourselves tough questions. For example: Is there an overriding purpose in my life, a purpose that is vivid and precise, a purpose I am committed to, a purpose that makes sense of everything I do?

It is sometimes helpful to recall the words of Ralph Waldo Emerson: "What is my job on the planet? What is it that needs doing, that I know something about, that probably won't happen unless I take responsibility for it?"

We can only identify this purpose by taking a hard look at ourselves, and giving ourselves the quiet time necessary to seek the answers. But answering the question of purpose begs other important questions.

For example: Am I going to allow my life to be controlled by the crush of daily activities, or will I live my life in accordance with my purpose?

Do day-to-day urgencies always have to shove higher-order concerns to the side? *Always*?

Sometimes a purpose and a career are incompatible, and something has to give. (I don't think one could be both a cop and a bank robber for very long.) But sometimes a particular purpose *can* be squared with a particular career. It may take nothing more than re-examining your career, asking some questions, and discovering a purpose you have overlooked in the past.

Here are three steps you can take on the road to self-knowledge:

Get to know yourself: You can't improve upon something you don't understand. The more questions you ask yourself, the better you'll know yourself.

Learn from failure: Failure can bring some of the toughest questions of all. If you answer them fully and honestly, you may learn more from failure than you do from success.

Don't run for the sake of running: Make sure you're headed somewhere. If you're going all out without a clear destination in mind, slow down and ask some more questions.

"I'm no better nor less than the next man. But the thing about me is that I always knew what my acts would mean. I was lucky ... I found a single-ness of purpose early on."

□ Be Guided by Convention

☑ Look the Truth Straight On

A key building block in the process of self-discovery is your willingness to look at the truth straight on. If you answer one or more of the tough questions mentioned in the first lesson without being fully honest, you gain nothing. Goals built on half-truths are almost certain to fail when push comes to shove. If you can't act on your convictions in a crunch, then success is out of the question.

A person who is grounded in truth doesn't have to look very far to find the right thing to do. When you are guided by the truth, you are the same person in private as you are in public. Looked at from the other end of the telescope, you know that what you do in private *matters*. Any talk of being able to "compartmentalize" your life, so that what you do in private has no bearing on your public life, is a fiction. Your principles only count if you *live* them, on and off the playing field.

If you're still not persuaded, consider this. As a leader, you can't build a team, department, or company that's a whole lot different from yourself—well, who are you? Do you want your company to have shaky foundations built on dishonest goals? If the answer is no, then make sure these things aren't part of you, either. The researcher can't help but influence what he's observing, and the inventor can't take himself out of his creation.

Honesty also plays an important role in the interactions between a leader and his organization. Without complete honesty, there can be no trust, and if your people don't trust you, you can't lead them. Trust is earned through patient investment and a consistent track record, and it can be destroyed in an instant. As a leader, you will be closely watched, and everything you say will have meaning for your people. Actions that contradict your message—or dishonest messages—will destroy trust and be used as an excuse not to take you seriously.

Here are three things to consider in your search for the truth:

Don't try to fake it: People have an unerring nose for dishonesty, fraud, and pretense. To be successful, you must be honest with yourself and others.

Expect to be observed: As a leader, you're being watched 24 hours a day, seven days a week. You can't build a team that's different from yourself, so be honest with yourself, and with your team.

Don't compartmentalize: Your conduct matters at all times. If you compromise your principles in your private life, it may well affect your public life, as well.

"The successful man is himself. To be successful, you've got to be honest with yourself."

☐ Fit Your Character to Others' Expectations

☑ Play to Your Strengths

Self-discovery is nothing if not personal, both in the process and in the results. There is no formula by which you can find out what makes you tick, no standardized test that will reveal your goals in life. Looking within yourself to ask the tough questions is an individual quest, and you must not conform to what you think the results should be.

The trick is to find your own strengths, and to play to those strengths. As you start to answer the questions that lead to self-knowledge, certain strengths—and weaknesses—in your own character will begin to become evident. (This is not a bad thing. Strong people tend to have strong weaknesses; as long as you're aware of them, they don't have to work to your disadvantage.) Good leaders will work to combat their weaknesses, and use their strengths to the greatest advantage.

There are many ways in which we may learn more about our own strengths and weaknesses. Some of these are techniques we can choose to practice, such as prayer, meditation, or long walks in the country. These are methods by which we *pay attention*, in very specific ways: with intention, in the present moment, and non-judgmentally. Keeping a journal can also be a way to learn more about yourself. Other learning experiences are less voluntary; pain, for example, can provide invaluable insights but is rarely a method that people would choose for themselves.

The important thing is to make the commitment to self-knowledge, through whatever means works for you, and to accept and use to your advantage the results of this discovery process. Coach Lombardi used to say that he was never successful using someone else's plays, and the same holds true in life, as in business. Your greatest strengths as a leader are those qualities that are unique to *you*.

As you discover them, use them to your advantage. Different people find their ways through different paths, and if you take someone else's path, you may not like where you end up.

Here are three ways to learn more about your strengths and yourself:

Choose your own path: It doesn't have to be the path less traveled, or the one of least resistance. What matters is that it's the right one for *you*.

It's not a failure if you learn something: Be open to the learning process. Whether it's pain, mistakes, or success, every experience can teach you something. Sometimes the hardest lessons are the most important.

Practice continuous renewal: Continuous, disciplined self-examination internalizes the lessons you're learning about yourself and allows you instinctively to play to your own strengths.

"What it will all come down to ... is that we will try to do what we do best. We ... will go with our strengths."

☐ ~~Let Circumstances Shape You~~

☑ Write Your Character

We come now to the second stage of the Lombardi model: character building. *Character* is the first requirement of Lombardi's leadership code. Combined with good habits and competence, character creates the building blocks for leadership.

Lombardi spoke often of character. His preseminary training, his rigorous education at the hands of Fordham's Jesuits, and his sustained immersion in what might be called the "secular religion" of West Point—where a code of duty and honor prevailed—were immensely influential. This sequence of educational experiences, consistently focused on values, helped him become the man he was. It made him unusually aware of how one goes about building character.

The word "character" is derived from older words that mean "engraved" and "inscribed." These etymological roots imply something important. Character is written, inscribed, and engraved all over you. Everyone has a character, but not all of us are "of" character. Character is founded on unchanging principles. It is your underlying core. It has unspoken power, it is solid and resolute, it doesn't blink.

Most important, character is a series of decisions and choices that you make as you grow and mature. Character is not something that is handed to you; it must be forged through years of hard work and discipline. It is the culmination of years of choosing to act one way rather than another, of choosing truth over deception, respect over arrogance, compassion over cruelty. There is not one prescription for character. A favorite theme of Lombardi's was that you cannot simply copy someone else's character. Character must fit our own personality and characteristics if it is to withstand trial by fire.

There are many techniques for "writing your character." These include the habits of seeking truth, finding and keeping faith, practicing humility, and showing respect and compassion for others. None is easy to adopt; all are important for leadership. Here are three techniques you can use as you write your character:

Learn from hardship: It is at the most difficult times that we become most open to profound learning. Sometimes when we realize we don't have all the answers, we begin to ask the right questions.

Building character takes discipline: Internalizing the principles and values that you believe in means that they will surface in times of crisis. This takes daily renewal and practice.

Identify your heroes: Heroes embody qualities of character that are important to us and compel us to examine more closely how we're conducting our own lives.

"Improvements in moral character are our own responsibility. Bad habits are eliminated not by others, but by ourselves."

☐ ~~Be Detail-Oriented~~

☑ Think Big Picture

Once you've begun to know yourself, the next step is to make sure that everything you do is directed to the successful completion of your goals.

Vince Lombardi's professional life was completely devoted to making his teams successful. He didn't tolerate outside interests interfering with his players' dedication to their game, and certainly wouldn't have put himself in that situation. As the Packers' general manager, he ran a tight ship, and he ran it conservatively. He dominated the Packers' executive board.

Lombardi found ways to compensate in areas where he didn't have much experience, especially at the outset of his professional coaching career. He was an effective delegator, and he didn't hesitate to ask questions when he didn't understand something—one sign of a confident leader—and he didn't tolerate answers that he considered half-baked. He ran tight, agenda-driven meetings, which began and ended on schedule.

All of these effective strategies allowed him to focus on the one overarching mission—winning football games. Victory on the field—whether the field in question is your marketplace or Lambeau Field—is in part the outgrowth of a comprehensive vision and strategy, based on a complete understanding of the leader's vision and strengths. And every part of the organization must be focused on this *big picture*.

This doesn't mean that the big picture doesn't change as the competitive environment changes. In fact, the ongoing viability of an organization depends on the adaptation of its mission to the current climate. But the big picture must not be affected by minor setbacks, or organizational hiccups.

Consider the following to keep the big picture in the forefront of your consciousness for you and your organization:

Link goals to vision: Goals must be anchored in conviction. Make sure that your goals are closely linked to your mission; if they aren't, it will be too easy to throw them overboard at the first sign of adversity.

Change with the competitive environment: The long-term viability of an organization depends on its ability to adapt to a changing environment. Sooner or later, your product will become obsolete. If you're not ready to take advantage of that moment, somebody will.

Don't be swayed by minor setbacks: Don't confuse minor shifts with sea-changes. A bump in the road can—and should—be navigated without making major route changes.

"The difference [between a good coach and an average coach] is knowing what you want, and knowing what the end is supposed to look like. If a coach doesn't know what the end is supposed to look like, he won't know it when he sees it."

☐ Keep Your Options Open

☑ Be Completely Committed

Lombardi had a clear vision of the characteristics that you must develop to build your character to become an effective and successful leader. First among equals in achieving this is *commitment*.

Total commitment implies a lack of concern for anything except the task at hand. Total commitment means no loafing, idling, standing around, goofing off, or phoning in sick. It means accepting sacrifice, suffering, hard work—in other words, whatever it takes to reach your goal.

The essence of commitment is the act of making a decision. The Latin root for decision is "to cut away from," as in an incision. When you commit to something, you are *cutting away* all your other possibilities, all your other options. When you commit to something, you are also cutting away all the rationalizations, all the excuses.

Coach Lombardi gave 100 percent effort, 100 percent of the time. (He also expected it.) He confessed that it was hard to define a 100 percent effort, beyond a simple statement: "It was all there was. There was nothing left." He said with conviction that he knew that kind of effort when he saw it. Upon arriving at Green Bay, he felt that perhaps half of the Packers gave 100 percent most of the time. To win a championship, he told them, they all had to give 100 percent, 100 percent of the time.

Lombardi was a man who believed in himself and his methods and saw victories as an affirmation of those methods. This singleness of purpose came in part from the fact that he had waited so long for the opportunity to be a head coach, to be the one in control. By the time he got the job he wanted—he was 46 when he got the Green Bay job—there was a lot of pent-up energy and determination to succeed.

Singleness of purpose—total commitment and intensity—is something all leaders can develop. Part of it lies in believing in what you're doing. Lombardi fervently believed that what he was doing was very important. Because of it, he radiated an intensity and commitment that was *electric*.

Here are three techniques to up the "commitment quotient" in your organization:

Start with yourself: Inspire those around you with your own level of commitment. When leaders go the extra mile, their troops will follow.

Talent only gets you so far: A person with 100 percent ability and 50 percent commitment can throw a wrench into the whole system through inattention, inconsistency, and laziness.

Weed out the uncommitted: The organization that wins is populated by winners. Weed out the uncommitted, and get the last 10 percent out of everyone else.

"I would say that the quality of each man's life is the full measure of that man's personal commitment to excellence and to victory—whether it be football, whether it be business, whether it be politics or government, or what have you."

☐ Work Harder Than the Next Guy

☑ Work Harder than Everybody

Don't buy the myth of the overnight success. Most of the people we celebrate for their effortless achievements have actually put a whole lot of energy into preparing for their victory. Yes, they make it look easy. And they may even talk in a way that makes their success seem almost inevitable. But if you listen to them, you'll usually find that they are describing their pursuit of a compelling goal. It's the clarity of that goal—vivid, precise, energizing— that makes their success seem predestined.

What they're *not* necessarily talking about, in the flush of victory, are the long lonely hours of practice that they subjected themselves to, or the many, many doubts they experienced along the way.

Vince Lombardi was always a hard worker. When he took the assistant coaching job at West Point under head coach Red Blaik, though, he got a new perspective on what constituted "hard work." Blaik lived and breathed football during most of his waking hours. It wasn't unusual for him to reassemble his coaching staff after dinner and to watch films and discuss strategies until midnight. Then they'd be at it again first thing in the morning.

Lombardi carried these habits forward with him into his professional career. "When the other coaches—the rest of us—would leave the Giant offices," head coach Jim Lee Howell of the New York Giants once recalled, "there was always one light still burning, the one in Vince Lombardi's office."

Lombardi placed great emphasis on practice. He and his assistants would run the same play over and over again with Lombardi barking out "Run it again!" each time there was even the tiniest mistake. After a while, it was the *players* who would yell, "Run it again!" With hard work, practice, and discipline, they were gaining complete confidence in their ability to execute this particular play. It is this discipline of hard word and training, investing those countless hours of practice, that leads to mastery, that takes a skill from the conscious level to just being the way you do things.

Here are three techniques to make sure you're working hard:

Perfect your discipline: Hard work is *discipline*: focused training that develops self-control. It helps you make the hard decisions, endure pain, and stay on track despite stress, pressure, and fear.

Invest in your talent: All too often, our culture celebrates success without effort. And all too often, these stories turn out to be untrue—there *has* been effort—or they celebrate a flash in the pan. You have a duty to invest in your talent, for the long-term.

Start at home: Lombardi's grueling schedule sent a message to his players. They all saw him put in more effort than they did, and therefore were motivated to put in more effort themselves.

"The harder you work, the harder it is to surrender."

☑ Be Prepared to Sacrifice

Lombardi often talked approvingly about the "Spartan" qualities of football. "When I speak of 'Spartanism,'" he explained, "I'm speaking not so much of leaving the weak to die, but I'm speaking of the Spartan quality of sacrifice, and the Spartan quality of self-denial."

Football distills and clarifies the choices that lie behind sacrifice. As Lombardi readily admitted, it's a violent game, which has to be played violently. It makes demands on players that aren't made in any other sport. It imposes pain and injury, and *fear* of pain and injury.

But pain and the fear of pain is no excuse to avoid sacrifice. When Lombardi first got to Green Bay, he found a lackadaisical attitude rampant among the players. After the first day of practice, he was completely discouraged. What could he do to turn this team around?

When he walked into the training room the next morning, he found it full of players getting treatment for a variety of minor ailments. He snapped. "Get this straight!" he barked. "When you're hurt, you have every right to be in here. You'll get the best medical attention we can provide. We've got too much money invested in you to think otherwise.

"But this has got to stop. You're going to have to learn to live with small hurts, and play with small hurts, if you're going to play for me. Now I don't want to see this again!" For the most part, he didn't.

Too often, we seek to protect and shield people from the pain and frustration of mistakes and failure. We say, "Don't bite off more than you chew," and, "Be happy with what you have." What a disservice we do to these people! *Teach* your people to reach for the stars. They may not come down with any, but they will come away with a whole lot more than they would have had they not tried. And they will learn a very valuable lesson: Without pain, turmoil, commotion, anxiety, stress, and tension, there is no growth, no change. *You must pay the price*.

Here are three ways to think about sacrifice:

Sacrifice leads to success: It's sacrifice, during all those hours of training, that equips you to hang in there against all odds. Sacrifice and self-denial lie behind every success.

Use failures as stepping stones: It hurts to fall short of a goal. However, when you use a failure to your advantage, it can become merely a stepping stone on the road to victory.

Pay the price: Greatness is worth the cost. Great achievements require courage, determination, drive, and a willingness to pay the price.

"I think you've got to pay a price for anything that's worthwhile, and success is paying the price. You've got to pay the price to win, you've got to pay the price to stay on top, and you've got to pay the price to get there."

☐ Avoid the Hot Seat

☑ Be Mentally Tough

Mental toughness was one of Lombardi's favorite topics. He believed it was one of the most important leadership skills.

In the Lombardi code, mental toughness is the ability to hold on to one's goals in the face of the pressure and stress. It's the glue that holds a team together when the heat is on, and it helps that team persevere just a little bit longer—which in many cases is just enough to outlast the opposition.

Mental toughness means seeking out the pressure that can't be avoided anyway, and being *energized* by it. It's not the ability to survive a mistake or failure; it's the ability to come back stronger from failure.

Lombardi's own brand of mental toughness dates back to his days at Fordham. He was an average football player, compared to some of the more talented players around him. He *played*, nonetheless, because of his pure determination. He once played an entire game with a cut inside his mouth that, after the game, required thirty stitches to repair.

That toughness was challenged, and I'd say reinforced, in subsequent years by professional frustrations. As mentioned earlier, he waited a long time for the opportunity to lead a college team (and that opportunity never came). Next he waited for a top slot in the pros. It was a long and painful drought, which he simply had to endure.

As a coach, Lombardi schooled his players in the mental approach to football, telling them, "Hurt is in the mind." Players that didn't learn mental toughness didn't last long in Coach Lombardi's world.

Mental toughness is not something that people are born with. Instead, it's learned. We start small, achieving a minor goal. Then we set our sights higher, and succeed again. If we work patiently, we will prevail. Each time we raise the ante, we gain skills and confidence that make the next success more likely. This cycle—hard work, success, more hard work, more success, with the occasional setback thrown in—is the crucible of character.

Here are three ways to develop mental toughness:

Keep the pressure on: Good leaders help their troops stay alert and focused. Keep the pressure on, but stay within individual and organizational breaking points.

Never give in: It's easy to do well when there's no pressure or stress, but how many of us can be poised when defeat is nipping at our heels? Mental toughness is not rigidity in the face of adversity; it's stability and poise in the face of challenge.

Work at it: Mental toughness is the willingness to keep commitments you make to yourself. It's singleness of purpose. It's the ability to stay motivated, no matter what obstacles arise in your path.

"The most important element in the character make-up of a man who is successful is that of mental toughness."

☐ ~~Assert Ego~~

☑ **Balance Humility and Pride**

For a leader, part of humility is the recognition that you get results only through the efforts of others. It is one way of embodying truth, and reinforcing character. An effective leader understands that even the most powerful person is only a bit player on the larger stage of life.

This is not to say that ego is bad. The progress of the human race has been built upon the egos of great statesmen, scientists, soldiers, industrialists, and educators. All good leaders have strong egos. Ego is a pride that pushes you to accept nothing less than your personal best because your name is on your effort. The more we believe in ourselves, the higher our self-esteem and the more tension and anxiety we can endure on the road to achieving our goals. Ego, therefore, is closely tied to performance.

Lombardi had a healthy ego, and it was a vital contributor to his success. In fact, it's hard to imagine a Vince Lombardi without an on-his-sleeve ego. Every time he assembled his team in the locker room, you saw it. Each time his team took the field, you saw it.

But the same ego that helps leaders achieve greatness can also cause their downfall. This is hubris: arrogance, an outsized sense of self-importance. Nothing will sink a leader faster than hubris. It is the kind of ego that wants the quick fix, the instant gratification. It is the kind of ego that causes leaders to dictate that others must walk the talk while they themselves don't.

Humility is knowing that as a leader, the only thing you can control is how you act, in the here and now. It is humbling to admit you can't control the past or the future. You may try to control the different forces at work in your office, but there will come a time when you will have communicated to your people what it is you want done. You will have pleaded, cajoled, inspired, threatened—and then you will hold your breath and ask yourself, "Are they going to do what I want them to do or not?" And at that moment, it's out of your control.

Do you successfully balance pride and humility? Here are several things to think about:

Pride is necessary: Pride is a determination to never do less than your best. As such, it is critical to a healthy organization.

Beware of hubris: Never lose sight of the dark side of ego—the ego that gets in the way of truth and therefore interferes with leadership.

Give credit where it's due: Humility is about giving credit where credit is due. If you did it, take the credit. If you had help, recognize those who helped you.

"Simplicity is a form of humility, and simplicity is a sign of true greatness. Meekness is a sign of humility, and meekness is a sign of true strength."

☐ Demand Integrity from Others

☑ Lead with Integrity

We have now arrived at the third part of the Lombardi code: *techniques to translate strength of character into successful leadership*. One of the first steps is making sure that your troops share your commitment and drive. And one of the best ways to do this is to lead with integrity, a trait Lombardi referred to as "character in action." Integrity is the manifestation of an unshakable set of principles— principles that you will not violate under any circumstances.

One reason Lombardi was able to extract an extraordinary effort from his players was that they understood that he was making an even *greater* effort. True, he wasn't experiencing the cuts and bruises that players were incurring daily on the practice field. But he pushed himself to the limit, just as he pushed them. He came early, left late, and almost never took a day off. He was leading with integrity, demonstrating the same commitment he demanded from his players.

Leaders have to impress who and what they are—on the people around them. This means that you *do what is right*. You do what you say. You conform to the values that you espouse. Your behavior is predictable, because you are consistent in your choices and your actions.

Integrity has a cost. You must weigh the depth of your commitment before you undertake to lead with integrity. You will be tested—by cynics, by those interested in the lure of short-term gains, by those interested more in style than in substance. You'll need to make sure that you have deep enough reserves to act, *consistently*, as a person of integrity. People will be watching what you *do*, rather than listening to what you say.

Lombardi also monitored the attitudes of his players. Attitudes should continue to improve as hard work pays off—especially after players have a couple of wins under their belts. When that didn't happen, and Lombardi decided that the situation couldn't be salvaged, he moved quickly to get rid of the "bad apple." Consider the following tactics to help you lead with integrity:

Live what you teach: Great leaders (and great coaches) win the hearts of their followers. They do so by being involved up to their necks, and making that commitment clear.

Let 'em see you sweat: Why should other people kill themselves for the organization if you, the leader, aren't the first one over the barricade?

Build accountability: Act your integrity. Take responsibility when you screw up, and take credit when you meet with success. And make sure this applies to everyone else.

"If you cheat on the practice field, you'll cheat in the game. If you cheat in the game, you'll cheat the rest of your life."

☐ Build Individual Pride

☑ Build Team Spirit

Another critical leadership technique is team-building. Lombardi believed that a team of people working together with discipline, singleness of purpose, and a commitment to excellence could prevail, no matter how heavily the odds were stacked against them. Team spirit, according to Lombardi, grows out of three interrelated elements: common goals, complementary skills and abilities, and mutual accountability.

Common goals create drive and energy. A team that hungers for the same outcome is a motivated team. Common goals foster the subordination of the individual will to the group will.

Complementary skills and abilities make football the great game that it is. People play (and watch) football to experience that elusive, perfect mix of brains, brawn, experience, and drive that somehow come together to produce a winner. Coming up with that mix, and motivating the players who contributed to it, is what separated Lombardi from all but a handful of his fellow coaches.

Mutual accountability grows out of complementary skills and abilities. Teammates ultimately end up playing for each other. A key component of the Lombardi system was getting each player to believe that every other player would do his part, expertly, each time he was called upon to do so. How? In part by getting each player to do his own part expertly, through relentless drilling in the fundamentals. By the time Coach Lombardi was done with you, you were saying to yourself: I'm talented, I'm skilled, and I'm fully prepared to perform my role on this particular play—*and so is everyone else on this line and in this backfield*.

Lombardi told his players exactly what he expected of them. He convinced them that they had everything they needed to succeed—the training, the preparation, and the skills. He emphasized that their job was worth doing. And in all of this, he created an atmosphere of togetherness, inclusiveness, and solidarity.

Here are three tactics you can use to nurture the sense of team in your organization:

Fit your game to the talents of your team: A team works together most successfully when each individual component is used to best advantage. Tailor your approach to fit the abilities of your team members.

Emphasize responsibility and loyalty: Teams depend on an extraordinary cohesiveness. Encouraging all members of an organization to support and aid other members in the pursuit of shared goals will strengthen this bond.

Focus on team success rather than personal glory: Strong team members place the interests of the team first, sublimating their personal visions of glory to the team's success. A good leader will encourage—and exemplify—this trait.

"Build for your team a feeling of oneness, of dependence upon one another, and of strength to be derived from unity."

☐ ~~Give Orders~~

☑ Explain the Whys

Lombardi often used the words "teaching" and "coaching" interchangeably. He was both coach and teacher of the Green Bay Packers. He was essentially a "molder" of men—which applies equally to teachers and coaches.

As both a teacher and a coach, Lombardi concentrated on the *whys*. "I never tell a player, 'This is my way, now do it,'" he once said. "Instead, I say, 'This is the way we do it, and this is why we do it.'" This is along the same lines as creating a shared vision for the organization. If your people know the larger goals, and see the connection between their daily individual effort and achieving these goals, their motivation—and their ability to succeed—will be greatly enhanced.

Lombardi taught to the bottom of the "class," going slowly enough—and being repetitive enough—so that *no one* was left behind. The rationale was simple: If somebody doesn't get the point of the lesson and makes a mistake in the game, the efforts of ten other people can be instantly negated. And in Lombardi's model of football, every man was required to think for himself. Coaches can find ways to cover up a player's physical shortcomings; they can't cover for a player's mental mistakes during the course of a game.

The risk in this style of teaching/coaching, of course, is that the top of the class—or even the teacher—will get bored. Lombardi avoided this in part by the simple force of his personality and convictions. He had a way of making even a routine task sound important, as if there *were* no routine tasks. He made mundane things compelling.

Practice sessions that might have been deadly in the hands of a less gifted teacher remained interesting—even in their umpteenth repetition. "I loved it," recalled Packers quarterback Bart Starr. "I never, ever was bored or tired at any meeting we were in with Lombardi. I appreciated what he was trying to teach. He was always trying to raise the bar."

Here are three ways to teach more effectively:

Teach to the slowest: The strategy must be crystal clear to everyone in the organization. This means drilling it until the slowest member of the team has it down.

Start with why, not how: People who understand why they're working will be better motivated and more successful. It's all about sharing the vision, on every level of the organization

Avoid boredom: Lombardi used the force of his personality. Use any means in your grasp to keep your people from boredom. Boredom sinks as many organizations as incompetence.

"They call it coaching, but it is teaching. You do not just tell them it is so, but you show them the reasons why it is so and you repeat and repeat until they are convinced, until they know."

☑ Strike the Balance

As you climb the ranks of the organizational hierarchy, the demands that the organization places upon you change in many ways—some obvious, some subtle. New titles, of course, bring new responsibilities. This is an obvious change. But new titles also bring, among other things, a change in the relationship between the leader and the led.

When Lombardi was an assistant coach with the Giants, he played golf with the players during the day and cards with them at night. Sometimes he had players over to the house for dinner. In Green Bay, however, as a head coach, Lombardi kept his distance from the players. Now he played golf and cards with friends from the local business community. He rarely socialized with his assistants. He was the *leader*.

This was a turn of events that Lombardi wasn't particularly happy about. One of the things he liked best about football was the close association with the players—the camaraderie. As an assistant, he was able to enjoy that easy relationship to the fullest. Not so, as head coach.

An interesting paradox emerged in the later stages of Lombardi's career. He didn't like the loneliness that came with leadership, but he took it to be an inevitable aspect of his job. At the same time, however, he was still intimately involved in the lives of several dozen young men. He may have been "distant," but he was still in contact. The head coach had many opportunities to stay in touch with his players.

This changed for the worse when he stepped down as Green Bay's head coach. Now he was a "leader"—in the sense of being a general manager—without the benefit of a coach's link to the lives of his players. It was a painful and abrupt transition, which he likened to losing a family. Eventually, his desire to recreate what he had lost led him to accept the Redskins' offer of the head coaching position.

Here are three things to consider as you strive to maintain a balance in your own organization:

Be as close as you can: Lombardi knew that a good leader *feels deeply* for his people and that he needs to let them know that he cares. This is an important way of building the mutual respect that every successful team requires.

Get ready to be lonely: When your position changes, some relationships will, too. Part of being a good leader is accepting the distance that this brings.

Familiarity breeds contempt: If you are too close to those under your command, your ability to lead may suffer.

"The leader can never close the gap between himself and the group. If he does, he is no longer what he must be. He must walk a tightrope between the consent he must win and the control he must exert."

☑ Build Confidence

Confidence means trusting in someone, and relying upon them. It also means self-reliance.

In the three years before Lombardi arrived in Green Bay, the Packers' won-loss records were 4-8, 3-9, and 1-10-1, respectively. Confidence would have been hard to find anywhere in the vicinity of Lambeau Field. Then something unexpected happened. In came a new coach, who stated flatly that he had never been part of a losing team and sure didn't intend to start *now*.

The players were overwhelmed by the quality of Lombardi's planning, and in the face of his assurances, found themselves suddenly believing in their own ability. That was exactly the impression that Lombardi was trying to create. What set him apart was his ability to make each player feel confident and believe in himself. Lombardi practically *oozed* confidence—in the forcefulness of his voice, his carriage, his very presence.

Projecting confidence was only stage-setting, of course. The real confidence-builder was *preparation*. Lombardi prepared his players for every game, for every eventuality. Going into a game, they believed that they would not encounter a situation that they weren't prepared to handle. Think of Julius Caesar's celebrated analysis of his legions: "Without training, they lacked knowledge. Without knowledge, they lacked confidence. Without confidence, they lacked victory." Success, in turn, brought more confidence, which brought more success. "You'd be surprised," Lombardi liked to say, "how much confidence a little success will bring."

Lombardi believed in his players. Because he believed in them, they came to believe in *themselves*. His success was built on the premise that the players could do what he demanded of them. He asked for confidence in his system, and convinced them that together they would succeed.

Here are three things you can do to improve the confidence level in your organization:

Project confidence: Confidence is catching, and so is a lack of confidence. If a leader exudes confidence, his troops will follow his lead.

Success breeds confidence: A team that starts winning immediately increases its confidence and immediately increases its chance of winning again.

Give people the tools they need: Set the stage psychologically, and give people the skills and tools they need to succeed. Preparedness is the ultimate confidence builder.

"You defeat defeatism with confidence. The man who is trained to his peak capacity will gain confidence. Confidence is contagious, and so is a lack of confidence."

☐ Use Your Authority

☑ Use Your Mission

What is your organization about? Why is your product or service worth buying? Who *cares* about your organization, and why? What do you collectively believe in? What's nonnegotiable? Where are you going?

To answer these kinds of core questions, you need to look at your *mission*. Mission is your company's reason to exist. It's who you are, what you do, and why you do it. It's what makes you unique. It's why you've all agreed to work together in a common cause. Without a mission you have no basis upon which to formulate your vision.

All of your organization's practices and decisions should correspond to the mission. If a proposed tactic or strategy is not in keeping with the mission, you don't do it—period. The mission is the standard against which everyone's actions are or should be judged.

Unfortunately, this is easier said than done. Judging a proposed action against the potential dollars-and-cents, bottom-line impact of that action is a tough enough challenge; judging such an action against a set of nonfinancial principles is even tougher. There are no easy answers—except to say that the mission must be clearly stated, and that everyone in the organization must be prepared and willing to assess action against the mission.

Sometimes the mission can be threatening to a leader. Total commitment to the mission means that there are real limits on the leader's authority. If the leader issues orders that circumvent or contravene the mission, the members of the organization are obligated to protect the mission against the leader. (Again, this is easier said than done!)

The Green Bay Packers' mission could be boiled down to a succinct sentence: "Winning isn't everything, it's the only thing." Everything the Packers did was judged against this mission: If the proposed action didn't contribute to winning, it wasn't done.

Here are three ways to use your mission:

Create a shared vision: Good leaders share the vision-creating task to broaden the base of ownership, to generate commitment, and to reduce the level of threat inherent in the planned change.

Link goals to purpose: In a healthy organization, all key decisions are put through the screen of the mission. If a proposed goal doesn't support the mission, change course.

Align your values: The leader's challenge is to bring *stated* and *practiced* values into alignment. The failure to do so leads to organizational cynicism—*we say it, but we sure don't do it!*—and undercuts the leader's moral authority and credibility.

"The man who succeeds above his fellow man is the one who early in life clearly discerns his objective, and towards that objective he directs all of his powers."

☑ Know Your Stuff

People who are in trouble, who are feeling rud-
derless, are inclined to cut a new leader some slack.
But the honeymoon lasts only so long. During that
honeymoon, the leader must demonstrate his or her
unquestioned competence.

By all accounts, Vince Lombardi knew his stuff.
When he became an assistant coach with the New
York Giants, the players initially had little respect for
him. After all, Lombardi hadn't even been a head
coach for a college team. Only seven years previous,
he had been coaching high school football. What
could he teach them?

Gradually, Lombardi proved himself to the players. He demonstrated his knowledge of every detail
of the game—where to step, how to throw, how
deep the guards ought to pull, and so on. Lombardi
had complete command of what he was teaching,

and as this became clear to the players, he also commanded their respect. He made the same impression upon his arrival in Green Bay: According to assistant coach Jerry Burns, he knew every part of the machine intimately.

Lombardi endured a long apprenticeship—high school, Fordham, West Point, and New York. He chafed at being in the assistant's position for so many years and resented being held back. But over all those years, he also achieved a level of mastery over his craft that few others ever attained. This mastery served him well when he finally got his opportunity. Coaches and players alike understood that Lombardi was unlikely to make naïve mistakes. And because he was so clearly competent, the occasional bad call—or bad break—never undercut his authority. This was critical to his leadership.

And finally, of course, the team began to *win*. Winning in football reflects the convergence of a lot of people's competence. And just as the leader is held primarily accountable for losses, he is also given credit for wins that are achieved on the field by others.

Here are several tactics to consider:

Demonstrate competence: When the time comes, show that you know it. Those under you will gain respect for and confidence in your leadership.

Build your skills from the bottom up: Even if you don't feel you're getting the visibility you deserve, continue to hone your skills and demonstrate your competence. Years of obscurity gave Lombardi the chance to improve his technique.

Import special skills: If there's someone out there who can complement your own skills and add value to the organization, grab him or her.

"A leader is judged in terms of what others do to obtain the results that he is placed there to get."

Share the Responsibility

☑ Demand Autonomy

When the Philadelphia Eagles offered Lombardi the head coach position in 1958, he was sorely tempted to accept. Eventually, though, he decided against taking the job. His friends persuaded him that he wouldn't have enough autonomy with the Eagles, whose ownership was badly fragmented.

When he took over as the coach at Green Bay, therefore, he was clearly focused on running his own show. The Packers organization agreed to let him serve as both coach and general manager—effectively giving him complete operating control.

At his first executive committee meeting in Green Bay, Lombardi made a startling announcement: "I want it understood that I'm in complete command. I expect full cooperation from you people, and you will get full cooperation from me in return." Part of his strategy here was to nip in the bud some bad habits that had taken root in Green Bay. In previous years, players had discovered that if they knew someone on the executive committee, they could sometimes translate that connection into more playing time.

He also wanted sufficient flexibility to build a winning organization *his* way. He was brimming over with energy and ideas about how to move the Packers forward, and he didn't want to risk realizing only half his vision. In order to make a difference, it had to be all or nothing.

By striking the right deal up front, he gave himself enormous latitude to make changes. This was truly a case in which a business turnaround was needed, and the Packers' executive committee had consciously gone out and hired what could today be called a "turnaround artist."

The specifics of one particular situation, of course, aren't replicable, but the generalizations behind the specifics are powerful. Develop a clear sense of the right opportunity. Understand your bargaining position. Bargain for *autonomy*. Give yourself enough elbow-room to let yourself survive the inevitable missteps in the initial phase.

Here are three things to consider when leading an organization:

Don't confuse control with dictatorship: Lombardi was not demanding unchecked authority, and still lived within the rules of the Packers' organization and the NFL. Although he sometimes disagreed with these organizations, he conducted himself as a subordinate when appropriate.

Fight special interests: Just as Lombardi's Packers couldn't dictate their own playing time, special interests shouldn't dictate strategy. If it's not in the organization's interest, fight it.

Delegate when necessary: Figure out what you *must* control, and control that. Look for non-critical operations where you already have strong help, and define them as somebody else's problem.

"If I were coaching and someone else in the organization were questioning me, I couldn't take that."

☑ Respect Legitimate Authority

Respect for authority was one of Lombardi's most deeply held beliefs. It stemmed from his seminary training, his education at the feet of the Jesuits, and his apprenticeship at West Point with coach Red Blaik. Legitimate authority deserves respect—and all the more so if you, yourself, represent authority.

Lombardi demanded absolute autonomy in his own organization, but he did submit to authority greater than his own. At one point in his career, a major press conference was scheduled on the eve of a championship game. Everyone showed up except the star of the show: Vince Lombardi. NFL employees reached him by phone at his nearby hotel. Lombardi said that since he hadn't been informed of the press conference and already had made other plans, he wouldn't be attending. Commissioner

Rozelle got on the phone. After a very brief conversation, Lombardi said he'd be right over.

A second example to the contrary illustrates the same point. Late in his career, when an official made a particularly bad call against the Redskins—"bad" in Lombardi's eyes, at least—he followed the offending referee into his dressing room at the end of the game to continue complaining about the call. This was strictly against league rules. Commissioner Pete Rozelle reprimanded Lombardi for his misbehavior, and expressed surprise that a coach who was "so personally dedicated to authority and respect for order" would flout the rules to such an extent. Rozelle later said that, based on Lombardi's chastened behavior in a subsequent meeting, he was convinced that this pointed criticism was far more effective than the usual fine would have been.

One foundation upon which this respect for authority was built was Lombardi's deep religious faith. Faith was the basis of his discipline, and the respect instilled by his Jesuit teachers—for his teachers and for God—had a lasting impact on his attitude toward authority.

Here are several ways to make sure authority is respected in your organization:

Lead by example: If you're going to ask people to respect your authority, you'll need to lead by example.

Maintain discipline: Respect for authority is discipline in another guise. As Lombardi said, "A disciplined person is one who follows the will of the one who gives the orders."

Respect the system: Whatever hierarchy you're in—assuming its authority is legitimate—deserves your respect.

"You gotta remember one thing: If you're going to exercise authority, you've got to respect it."

☑ Act, Don't React

Experience is a wonderful teacher.

An important caveat, however, is that leaders must be willing to learn from their choices. If they don't, the experience becomes nothing more than repetitive motion. Leaders who don't learn from experience may recreate some successes—but they are equally likely to make the same *mistakes*, over and over again.

Sometimes, in looking to learn from the past, we scan our past experiences to characterize the present stimulus. Then we react, out of habit, much the same way we reacted the last time we faced a similar experience. But often, a mechanism we developed to handle and cope with a situation in the past is inappropriate for the current circumstance. So letting the past influence how we act in the present may prove a detriment.

For a leader, real power arises in that moment between a stimulus and then *choosing not* to react in the habitual way. By seizing that moment—by choosing to *act*, rather than react—the leader can effect real and positive change.

Coach Lombardi valued experience, and he studied the past to discover the truth. As he prepared to play a particular opponent, he would study films of previous games the Packers had played against that team, as well as the film of that team's game the previous week.

But Lombardi and his staff also knew that relying too heavily on past experience was dangerous. What had worked in the past against this opposing team might not work this week, because the other team's coaches were also making adjustments, and looking to create some sort of edge for their players.

So Lombardi also made sure that his team was ready to take action in the present. In pro football—as in business—living in the past was a prescription for defeat. The championship team that dwelled on last year's championship was unlikely to repeat that achievement.

Here are three techniques to help you act in a new situation rather than react:

Study the past, live in the present: Find yesterday's lessons, but assume that today is new.

Continue learning: The best way to be ready for the challenges of tomorrow is to keep learning today. Relying on the old skills that have worked in the past will backfire, as those skills become obsolete.

Seize the moment: Seize the initiative by seeing things for what they are ... and act without hesitation on what you see.

"While statistics are interesting, they're all in the past."

☐ ~~Innovate at Any Cost~~

☑ Keep It Simple

Vince Lombardi's playbook was simpler and short-er than those of most other coaches. He didn't ask his players to commit dozens of complicated plays to memory. Instead, he expected his players to mas-ter a small number of plays thoroughly. He would diagram each play painstakingly, painting a clear pic-ture for his players of what each play would look like when every player did his job flawlessly.

Once these basic plays became second nature, he asked his players to become equally familiar with a dozen or more *options* that might be run off each of those core plays. Suddenly, the playbook includ-ed "hundreds" of plays—but they were organized logically and simply in each player's mind as collec-tions of related options. Simple, but innovative.

Flexibility, intersected by discipline, was the key. The book that Lombardi wrote in 1963 with W. C. Heinz—*Run To Daylight!*—took its title from the tactics employed by the Packer running backs to make the celebrated "Packer sweep" and other plays work. Simply put, rather than running toward a designated spot in the line and hoping that the offensive lineman would open a hole, the back "ran to daylight"—going with the play as called and following his blockers, but also looking for an unexpected opening in the defense to run to *daylight*.

Lombardi was loath to depart from his game plan. He acknowledged the inevitability of change, and believed that leaders who refused to innovate would sooner or later be swept out with the tide. But fundamentally, he believed in playing to one's strengths. Adjustments should be made only at the margins of your game. Rather than departures from the playbook, they should only be refinements upon it.

This isn't a universal prescription, and it works better for an organization that's already successful than one that's struggling: A struggling organization may have to innovate every which way (and may still flounder). But your innovations still have to reflect people's limited capacities to learn and to change. Be fair and realistic.

Here are three tactics to keep your organization simple:

Play to your strengths: Only a grossly inferior organization should ever deviate from its strengths to win. Offensive forays should be based on rapidity of maneuver, not radical change.

Innovate without complicating: Change is inevitable. But don't change for the sake of change. Make adjustments at the margins of your game, and remember to keep them simple.

Stress depth over breadth: People who understand one area in depth are likely to be more effective than those who cover lots of acreage superficially.

"Almost always, the plan is too complex. Too much to learn and perfect in too little time."

☑ Chase Perfection

Lombardi often said that he believed in catching stars and was willing to take his chance on a hernia. This statement, although half in jest, illustrates one of the most crucial lessons in the Lombardi code: A good leader encourages people to reach beyond what they believe is possible. Though perfection may be unattainable, aiming high will allow people to surpass their own preconceived limitations.

Striving for perfection is more than simply an organization objective. According to Coach Lombardi, it was also an obligation for anyone who possessed talent. A frequent locker room topic of conversation concerned using talents to their fullest. Anyone who didn't, according to Lombardi, was cheating—on their God, on themselves, and on the team.

Lombardi insisted on excellence up and down the Packer organization and in every aspect of the team's performance. He believed that wanting to excel was a human constant, and he understood the importance of setting extremely high standards and never relaxing those standards.

Football, like every other field of endeavor, has its elite, based on excellence in execution. This excellence is achieved by the relentless pursuit of perfection. Lombardi considered excellence to be an attainable by-product of the quest for perfection. He thought of this quest—whether as a coach or a player—as both necessary and frustrating.

Leaders must choose *how* their organizations will pursue excellence. There are many models to choose from, and although Lombardi never learned or used the jargon of contemporary organizational theory, he employed many different techniques. He understood that some people, the great ones, are self-motivated to be their best. Others are motivated by the goal of beating the competition. Still others take their greatest satisfaction from being a part of a successful team effort. The task of any leader is to determine what motivates each individual. Not everyone responds the same. The leader must find each person's "hot button."

Here are three techniques for chasing perfection:

Aim for the stars: When people are encouraged to reach beyond their grasp, the results can be eye-opening. Successful leaders don't buy into perceived limitations.

Insist on excellence: The importance of setting high standards cannot be overestimated. And this can't be a part-time preoccupation.

The closer you are to the goal line, the more perfect you must be: Perfection matters most when the pressure is greatest—in those situations that can change the direction of an organization. At these moments, in particular, aiming for perfection pays dividends.

"If you settle for nothing less than your best, you will be amazed at what you can accomplish in your life."

☑Tailor Your Motivation

Great teams, like great organizations, are groups of talented individuals who subordinate their personal styles and goals to those of the team. But even the most disciplined teams—I'm thinking of the Packers under Lombardi, and the Boston Celtics under the legendary Red Auerbach—are still a collection of individuals, who need to be treated as individuals. Lombardi was a master of this critical leadership art.

Lombardi carefully distinguished among his players, feeding individual egos without pitting one teammate against another. One technique he used was a formal "grading system." Grades for individual performances on Sunday were posted the following Thursday, and in a mock-serious team ceremony, Lombardi handed out five-dollar bills (and later, ten-dollar bills) to the highest performing individuals. The Green Bay Packers players weren't overpaid, but they didn't need the money.

What they needed—what every individual needs—is to be recognized, by their leader and their peers, for outstanding individual performances. Part of the art of motivating individuals lies in doing your homework. Lombardi (whom Green Bay star Max McGee once referred to as "the greatest psychologist") tried to learn everything possible about the emotional make-up of his players, and then use that knowledge to its best effect. This meant treating every player fairly but differently.

Ultimately, leadership comes down to doing the hard, difficult things. You have to continually test your people. What motivates and inspires them? How much pressure can you apply? Will the players align with the vision? You will be called upon to do things that are unpopular. If you want to be popular, you won't push as hard, because you don't want people to dislike you. But if you don't push your people beyond their own perceived limits, you're not being an effective leader.

Here are three motivational tactics to consider:

Don't try to be popular: The desire to be liked interferes with the hard decisions a leader must make.

Counter expectations: Sometimes, the least expected motivational device is the best.

Keep the pressure on: Sooner or later, every organization will be in their version of a championship game. A good leader determines how their people will perform in pressure situations, and works with them to increase their tolerance for pressure.

"You can't coach without criticizing, and it's essential to understand how to criticize each man individually.... Football is a pressure business, and on my teams I put on most of the pressure. The point is that I've got to learn 40 ways to pressure 40 men."

Make It All or Nothing

☑ Motivate by Degrees

Motivation is not a one-step fix. It's not a one-game season; it's a sixteen-game season, plus the playoffs. It involves *reinforcement*, and a process of *adaptation* to new ways of thinking. As a leader, you must break down this "season of adaptation" into manageable parts. You need to create momentum—creating short-term wins to give credibility and staying power to your vision.

If in the summer of 1959, Coach Lombardi had talked exclusively about a world championship to a 1-10-1 team, he would have lost them. He would have been too far out in front. Talking "championship" would have been *demotivating*.

Lombardi understood that winning a championship would be but the last in a series of victories. To win the NFL Championship, the Packers needed to win the conference championship. To win the conference championship they had to win their division. To win the division title, they needed to win more games than the other teams in their division.

Over the course of a long season, victories come in all kinds of shapes and sizes. Victory in a particular game, for example, requires the accomplishment of goals on offense, defense, and special teams. Goals are further broken down by position. Linemen have goals for the game, as do the receivers, the quarterback, running backs, and the defense. Every player, moreover, has a goal for each play.

Coach Lombardi preached that most games are won by only a few specific plays. Since no one knew which play was going to win the game, each player had to give 100 percent on *every* play.

Winning the championship, therefore, had to be built on the foundation of a thousand small victories. It depended on each player seeing the connection between his daily individual effort and winning the championship. And it depended on motivation and inspiration by degree: people being encouraged by each small victory to move on to the next challenge.

Here are three techniques to help you motivate by degrees:

Begin with small victories: Small victories are a better beginning than visionary failures. Again, patience is crucial. Success must be built on strong foundations … and large victories on small ones.

Give frequent feedback: In order to keep striving, people must see that their efforts are producing results. Good leaders find small victories—and celebrate them publicly.

Be patient: A bottom-dwelling team doesn't become championship material overnight. A good leader is patient in both victory and defeat.

"This is not easy, this effort, day after day, week after week, to keep them up, but it is essential. Each week there is a different challenge, but there is also that unavoidable degree of sameness to these meetings."

☐ Concentrate on Expertise

☑ Focus on Fundamentals

Lombardi was a firm believer in the importance of fundamentals. Yes, there's always the chance that the stray fumble will break the game open, either in your favor or against it; but absent that, a good offensive line will win the game for you every time. This prescription applies to most businesses, as well. Help your front line people, your sales force, your engineers, and the rest is likely to follow.

Ball control is the most basic element of football. As long as you hold the ball, your opponent can't score. A business corollary is probably, "Define the turf on which you choose to compete. Stay on the offense; don't fall back to defense. Make your competitors react to you, rather than the other way around."

It's fundamentals—and their repetition, over and over again—that make for the win. Again, the parallels to business are pretty straightforward. *Stick to your knitting*. You never know when the critical moment in the competition is about to happen; when it arrives, you must be playing at the top of your game.

This has parallels up and down the line in business. Consider, for example, product design and engineering, or manufacturing quality control. Only a consistent standard of excellence will allow you to survive and prosper. Or take another kind of crisis: When a corporation faces a crisis of public confidence in its products or practices, the company simply has to be at the top of its game. It has to think clearly, move quickly and effectively, put out the fire, and stay in the game.

Although Lombardi was a believer in the fundamentals, he liked a good razzle-dazzle play as much as any coach. But *discipline* remained the watchword. There were many games in which the Packers faced desperate circumstances—down by more than a field goal, with only minutes to play—when the team marshaled the offense, worked the clock, and moved the ball down the field. They did it by being confident and relying on the fundamentals.

Here are three ways to focus on the fundamentals:

Build skills: Skills are the building blocks of any organization. You can't put big demands on people before you define and provide the needed skills.

Rely on repetition: Execution depends on confidence, and confidence depends on preparation. Only after the fundamentals become second nature can you be confident of the results.

Be prepared to seize opportunity: If there are only a small number of big plays in the course of a game (or in the life cycle of a product), you have to be functioning at a high level of excellence in order to take full advantage of those opportunities.

"I believe that if you block and tackle better than the other team and the breaks are even, you're going to win."

☐ Run with Style

☑ Run to Win

Winning is the ultimate goal in Lombardi's leadership model, and the ultimate consequence of your leadership abilities.

Lombardi is well known for the observation, "Winning isn't everything, it's the only thing." Actually, that famous statement originated with UCLA football coach Red Sanders ... but at the end of the day, it's not far off from Lombardi's philosophy. In many ways, he was absolutely right when he told his players that winning was the only thing. Especially during his first year or two in Green Bay, he was giving them good career advice.

A CEO coming into a turnaround situation would be well advised to consider saying something along the same line, emphasizing results: *This organization is in deep trouble. Either we all produce, or we're all out of here.* And even after the immediate crisis is past, that same CEO might keep reminding people on a regular basis that no organization has a guaranteed right to exist. *Yesterday doesn't matter; we're only winners if we win today.*

In the last analysis, it's results that define a leader. Management books are full of the debate about organizational structure—hierarchical or flat, centralized or decentralized, divisional or non-divisional, and everything in between. Yet it's not structure, but *results*, that prove a leader's methods. Leadership is not a position, it's a process that produces the desired results. If you don't produce results fairly, and squarely within the rules—if you can't execute—you are not a leader.

Leaders get paid for results, not for never making a mistake. If you seem to never make a mistake, you are not taking enough risks. Results require a willingness to act, even if you are unsure of what lies ahead. Only through action and taking calculated risks can you take your company to the next level. Results, specific and measurable, come from having a clear vision, defining what improvement and adaptation look like, and having a beginning and end in mind.

In the end, on the football field, on the factory floor, and in the corporate board room, results are the only thing that matters, and the desired results—the "win"—should be pursued with every ounce of the organization's energy and commitment.

Consider the following in your pursuit of victory:

Results are everything: Sometimes the leader has to make the obvious point: *If we don't win, we're out of business*. This focuses the team and fights complacency.

Win by the rules: Always work at winning but always play by the rules. Football—and business—would be anarchy without universally accepted guidelines for playing the game.

Understand the dangers of winning: If winning comes too hard, your team may get demoralized. If it comes too easily, it will be harder to stay motivated. Make sure you have a personal and organizational plan for the day after you succeed.

"The will to excel and the will to win—they endure. They are more important than any events that occasion them."

"I firmly believe that any man's finest hour, the greatest fulfillment of all that he holds dear, is the moment when he has worked his heart out in a good cause and lies exhausted on the field of battle—victorious."

A Game Plan for the Trainer and/or Human Resource Professional

Vince Lombardi believed first and foremost that leaders are *made*, not born. *The Lombardi Rules* was written with this important principle in mind. While the book is meant to be informative and inspirational, *The Rules* is first and foremost a leadership model.

There are a number of ways that you can use the model to build more effective leaders in your organization.

Give a copy of **The Rules** *to every leader and potential leader in your group or division with a personal note from you or the individual's manager.* This book is meant to be a stand-alone guide. It needs no additional explanation to achieve its goal of detailing a thought-provoking leadership model. However, it might be useful to include a note emphasizing that self-knowledge is the first step towards leadership, and how *The Rules* is designed to lead to greater self-knowledge.

After giving out **The Rules***, schedule a meeting or series of meetings to discuss and flesh out the leader-*

ship model. These meetings could be informal brown bag lunches to a full day, off-site session. In addition to discussing the content in the book, these sorts of sessions afford the group a rare opportunity to engage in a healthy and vigorous debate over the topic of leadership (which is an amorphous topic for many). It will also provide you an opportunity to observe leaders and future leaders in action.

Additionally, these meetings can help provide a platform in which you can build that sometimes elusive but critical organizational quality called "team spirit." In the Lombardi leadership model, team spirit emerges from the three interconnected elements of common goals, complimentary skills, and mutual accountability.

Common goals. In these team meetings it is always useful to outline those key goals that everyone must commit to if your organization is going to rise to the next level of success. Unless every member of the team understands what constitutes genuine success, it will make your task of taking the group to the next level all the more difficult.

Complimentary skills and abilities. The meetings will also provide you with a chance to gauge the strengths and weaknesses of your leaders. In settings such as these, in which all are encouraged to speak out, you may be surprised by which members of your group rise to the occasion.

Mutual accountability. These leadership sessions can also create within your organization a cohesiveness and a togetherness that will give rise to mutual accountability and responsibility.

If your group is relatively large (say, more than thirty or so participants), then you may opt to include breakout sessions as well. Here's how that could work:

- First meet as a group, explaining why you are getting together, the purpose of the meeting, as well as the other items mentioned above.
- Then, break the group into smaller units by having them count off in succession. For example, if you have thirty-five participants, then perhaps five groups of seven or so members would work nicely. Have them each count off 1 to 7. Then all the 1s get together as Team 1, the 2s as Team 2, and so on.
- Each team will need a team leader. Allow each team to figure that out for themselves, so that the high potential leaders emerge naturally from the process. Make sure to stress the importance of everyone being involved; leave no participant behind.
- Lastly, start with "why," not "how." That's a key part of the Lombardi formula. Coach Lombardi always emphasized:

"I never tell a player, 'this is my way, now do it.' Instead, I say, 'This is the way we do it, and this is why we do it.'"

Always keep the meetings interesting and dynamic. Avoid boredom. If you believe in what you are doing, the force of your belief and your enthusiasm for the concepts contained in *The Rules* will make these sessions compelling. Most of all, have fun. These sessions should be a welcome relief from the typical day-to-day grind. As long as the meetings are taken seriously, it isn't wrong to lighten things up with a bit of levity.

Other Titles in the McGraw-Hill Professional Education Series

The Welch Way: 24 Lessons from the World's Greatest CEO
by Jeffrey A. Krames (0-07-138750-1)

The Powell Principles: 24 Lessons from Colin Powell, the Legendary Leader
by Oren Harari (0-07-141109-7)

How to Motivate Every Employee: 24 Proven Tactics to Spark Productivity in the Workplace
by Anne Bruce (0-07-141333-2)

The New Manager's Handbook: 24 Lessons for Mastering Your New Role
by Morey Stettner (0-07-141334-0)

The Handbook for Leaders: 24 Lessons for Extraordinary Leadership
by John H. Zenger and Joseph Folkman (0-07-143532-8)

Leadership When the Heat's On: 24 Lessons in High Performance Management

by Danny Cox with John Hoover (0-07-141406-1)

How to Manage Performance: 24 Lessons for Improving Performance

by Robert Bacal (0-07-143531-X)

Dealing with Difficult People: 24 Lessons for Bringing Out the Best in Everyone

by Dr. Rick Brinkman and Dr. Rick Kirschner (0-07-141641-2)

How to Be a Great Coach: 24 Lessons for Turning on the Productivity of Every Employee

by Marshall J. Cook (0-07-143529-8)

Making Teams Work: 24 Lessons for Working Together Successfully

by Michael Maginn (0-07-143530-1)

Why Customers Don't Do What You Want Them to Do: 24 Solutions to Overcoming Common Selling Problems

by Ferdinand Fournies (0-07-141750-8)

The Sales Success Handbook: 20 Lessons to Open and Close Sales Now

by Linda Richardson (0-07-141636-6)

About the Author

Vince Lombardi Jr. has built successful careers in law, politics, sports, motivational speaking, and writing. A winner of the American Speakers Bureau's Speaker of the Year Award, Lombardi served in the Minnesota legislature while maintaining a private law practice and has held executive positions with the Seattle Seahawks, the NFL Management Council, and the United States Football League. He is the author of *What It Takes to be #1* and *The Essential Vince Lombardi*.